Making a Law

by Barbara Magalnick

PEARSON

Scott
Foresman

Editorial Offices: Glenview, Illinois • Parsippany, New Jersey • New York, New York
Sales Offices: Needham, Massachusetts • Duluth, Georgia • Glenview, Illinois
Coppell, Texas • Sacramento, California • Mesa, Arizona

Voting Rights in the Constitution

The United States holds an election for **President** every four years. Some countries do not vote for a president. Many countries do not even have a president!

When our Constitution was written in 1787, it included laws about voting and **freedom**. The Constitution is a paper that tells how our country is run. States had the right to add laws about who could vote.

Thomas Jefferson   James Madison

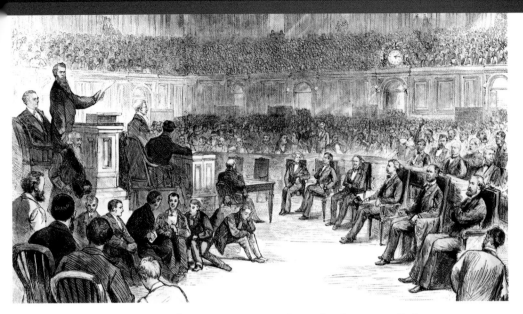

Electors in each state vote for their candidate.

The Electoral College

The writers of the Constitution set up a special way of choosing the President. When people vote, they see the names of the candidates. People, however, are actually choosing people to vote for them.

After the presidential election, the electoral college meets. These are the electors in each state. The winner of the most electoral votes becomes President.

George Washington, our first President

If You Want to Be President

The writers of the Constitution spent a lot of time thinking about who could be President. In the Constitution, they said that the President has to be at least thirty-five years old.

The writers of the Constitution thought the President should be elected for four years. The President also has to be an American **citizen**.

Americans Go West

During the 1800s many people came to the United States. At the same time people began to move west into land that was not yet settled. The pioneers traveled in wagons pulled by horses or oxen. There were many dangers on these long trips.

Pioneers had to work hard. The pioneer women in the West were among the first to be allowed to vote.

The pioneers had a long, hard trip across the country. They were looking for farmland.

The North and South Do Not Agree

The United States became divided. The northern states had large cities and factories. The southern states had many farms.

There were plantations in the South. Enslaved people often worked in the fields and houses.

The northern states wanted to end slavery in the South. Some southerners did not want the North telling them what to do. They wanted to decide about slavery themselves.

There were some large plantations in the South.

Abraham Lincoln began to end slavery when he signed the Emancipation Proclamation.

Important Amendments

An amendment is a change to the Constitution. The 13th Amendment ended slavery in the United States. The 14th Amendment made each former enslaved person a citizen. The 15th Amendment allowed them to vote.

Voting Is Not an Easy Right to Practice!

Some states made it almost impossible for African American men to vote. Some laws made men pay a tax in order to vote. People also had to show they could read and write, but it had been against the law for enslaved people to learn these skills.

The 15th Amendment gave African American men the right to vote.

There were also laws that said if a man's father or grandfather had been enslaved, he could not vote. Only the small number of African American men in northern states got to vote.

Women Work to Get to Vote

Some men were allowed to vote, but women did not have the same rights. For many years Susan B. Anthony and Elizabeth Cady Stanton worked hard to change this. They had a difficult time! The women and their helpers were often called names, and once Anthony was even sent to jail!

Elizabeth Cady Stanton and Susan B. Anthony worked hard telling people that women should be allowed to vote.

Western States Let Women Vote

When the Civil War ended, more people chose to go west. Railroads were being built to go all the way to California. Families cleared land for farms. Women and men worked in the fields. Women in the West were among the first to be given voting rights.

Women worked in factories during World War I.

Women Work and Vote

During World War I, women worked in factories and on farms while the men were away fighting. Most women had to give up their jobs when the men came home from the war. Seeing women work made people think about women's right to vote.

Changing the Constitution

Since many states would not let women vote, the Constitution would have to be changed by adding an amendment. Adding an amendment can take a long time. First, **Congress** must approve it. Then it is sent to the states. The 19th Amendment to the Constitution was passed by Congress in 1919. It was approved in 1920! Women could now vote for President.

Voting Rights for All!

During the 1960's people asked if our laws were fair to everyone. In 1964 the 24th Amendment to the Constitution said taxes could not be used to keep anyone from voting. In 1965 Congress passed the Voting Rights Act. It allowed the federal **government** to make sure states did not keep anyone from voting. Everyone could now vote!

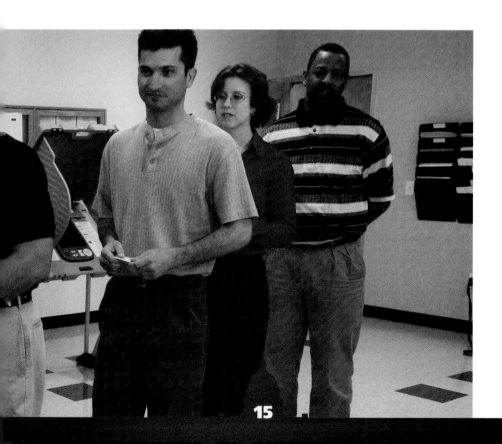

Glossary

citizen a member of a country

Congress the part of the United States government that writes and votes on our laws

freedom every citizen's right to make choices

government a group of people who work together to run a city, state, or country

President the leader of our country